Frédéric Chopin, James Huneker
40 Kompositionen für Klavier von Frédéric Chopin

Frédéric Chopin, James Huneker

40 Kompositionen für Klavier von Frédéric Chopin

ISBN/EAN: 9783956980961

Auflage: 1

Erscheinungsjahr: 2015

Erscheinungsort: Norderstedt, Deutschland

Hergestellt in Europa, USA, Kanada, Australien, Japan
Europäischer Musikverlag in Hansebooks GmbH, Norderstedt

FORTY PIANO COMPOSITIONS
FRÉDÉRIC CHOPIN
EDITED BY
JAMES HUNEKER

OLIVER DITSON COMPANY
THEODORE PRESSER CO., Distributors, 1712 CHESTNUT ST., PHILADELPHIA

CONTENTS

PRELUDE
in C. Op. 28, No. 1 — 1
in G. Op. 28, No. 3 — 2
in E Minor. Op. 28, No. 4 — 4
in B Minor. Op. 28, No. 6 — 5
in D♭. Op. 28, No. 15. (The Raindrop) — 6

MAZURKA
in B♭. Op. 7, No. 1 — 10
in B♭ Minor. Op. 24, No. 4 — 12
in D♭. Op. 30, No. 3 — 16
in G♯ Minor. Op. 33, No. 1 — 19
in C. Op. 33, No. 3 — 20
in B Minor. Op. 33, No. 4 — 22
in A♭. Op. 50, No. 2 — 27
in A Minor. Op. 68, No. 2 — 30

STUDY
in G♭. Op. 10, No. 5. (The Black Keys) — 33
in A♭. Op. 25, No. 1. (The Æolian Harp) — 37
in C♯ Minor. Op. 25, No. 7 — 42
in G♭. Op. 25, No. 9. (The Butterfly) — 46
in D♭ — 48

NOCTURNE
in E♭. Op. 9, No. 2 — 50
in F♯. Op. 15, No. 2 — 53
in D♭. Op. 27, No. 2 — 57
in B Major. Op. 32, No. 1 — 62
in G Minor. Op. 37, No. 1 — 65
in G. Op. 37, No. 2 — 69

WALTZ
in E♭. Op. 18. (*Grande Valse Brillante*) — 75
in A♭. Op. 34, No. 1. (*Valse Brillante*) — 83
in A Minor. Op. 34, No. 2 — 92
in A♭. Op. 42. (*Grande Valse*) — 97
in D♭. Op. 64, No. 1 — 105
in C♯ Minor. Op. 64, No. 2 — 109
in A♭. Op. 64, No. 3 — 115
in E Minor. (Posthumous) — 120

POLONAISE
in C♯ Minor. Op. 26, No. 1 — 124
in A Major. Op. 40, No. 1. (*Polonaise Militaire*) — 128

IMPROMPTU I
in A♭ Major. Op. 29 — 133

FANTAISIE-IMPROMPTU
in C♯ Minor. Op. 66. (Posthumous) — 140

BALLADE III
in A♭ Major. Op. 47 — 148

SCHERZO II
in B♭ Minor. Op. 31 — 159

BERCEUSE
in D♭ Major. Op. 57 — 175

FUNERAL MARCH (*Marche Funèbre*)
from the Sonata. Op. 35, No. 2 — 181

FRÉDÉRIC FRANÇOIS CHOPIN

(1809-1849)

FRÉDÉRIC CHOPIN

FRÉDÉRIC François Chopin is the greatest composer of music for the pianoforte. All that had been said before him by the masters, Bach, Mozart, or Beethoven, seems, after listening to Chopin, as if written in a language foreign to the instrument. When he speaks, it is the speech of one for whom this combination of wood, wire, iron and ivory is a human harp—a harp from which the most exquisite, sombre, tragic poetry is plucked. This Pole is rightfully named the poet of the keyboard—a title that has been often debased by claims of lesser men. He is first the poet, then the musician; and his achievements as musician are of such rare distinction as to give him a niche in the Pantheon of illustrious composers.

As was the case with his friend Franz Liszt, Chopin's skill as a pianoforte virtuoso overshadowed his genuine merits as a composer during his too short life. He was a wonderful pianist and he played his own music. This bewildered his contemporaries; the critics often failed to distinguish between his two gifts. If he played so marvellously, it was argued, not without justice, perhaps his music will not sound as beautiful under other fingers. But it did, and this is one of the tests of its universality; Liszt, Rubinstein, Tausig, Joseffy, Pachmann, Paderewski, and Rosenthal all played and play Chopin beautifully, while sects of warring critics, wrangling amateurs, cry "this is so," or "that is not so"; and yet no one may claim the unique Chopin tradition for the very simple reason that no such elusive quality exists. There is no Chopin tradition. There never was one, even when Chopin lived, for he played his compositions no two days, or ways, alike. This constitutes the evanescent, mysterious, poetic charm of his music; its secret has never been unriddled. And never will it be, for his is great art and great art always plays the *rôle* of the Sphinx to its eager votaries.

There is one right way to interpret Chopin. Plastic, entirely dream-like in its loveliness, his music yields only to the embrace of the poet. It may be wooed but never taken by assault. The poetry inherent in its structure, even in its technical figuration, sets it apart, a consecrated thing. To attack Chopin with burly fingers or sledge-hammer wrists is to destroy the aroma of his measures. As a poet he ranks with Shelley in the tenuity of his musical textures, in the supreme loftiness of his lyric flights; and he is twain with Keats in the richness of his harmonic coloring, in the deep-hued humanity of his melodic utterances. Therefore we think of him first as a poet.

As a musician Chopin took up the threads of that skein which antedates Mozart, Haydn, and Philipp Emanuel Bach. He found piano music given over to the empty formalism of Hummel or to the brilliant and inutile passage work of Kalkbrenner. By nature an aristocrat, the young Pole did not disdain the graceful framework of Hummel nor the elegant rhetoric of Kalkbrenner. But he had something new to say; they had not. He was a native of old Sarmatia and the patriot in him was mightily stirred by his nation's songs and nation's wrongs. He found near at hand simple dance forms and straightway, filled with eloquent music, idealized them; yet they lost not their native flavor, their wood-note wild. A sworn classicist in his devotion to Bach and Mozart, he is still the prince of the Romantics; a severe formalist, though his forms were not those of fugue or sonata, he nevertheless set beating the pulse of Europe with his gay valses and sparkling mazurkas. At his cradle had stood the Angel of Melancholy. No one ever heard Chopin laugh. His smile, rare and charming, was like that of his American brother-poet, Edgar Allan Poe. Both men were foredoomed to unhappiness; both disdained mediocrity and therefore supped their fill of misery.

II

Chopin was born in Zelazowa-Wola, six miles from Warsaw, Poland, March 1, 1809. He died in Paris October 17, 1849. But in those brief forty years, in the interval, as Walter Pater has it, he lived an existence devoted to art, a life that literally burned away his frail frame. By no means the delicate, effeminate child of the sentimental biographer, the little Frédéric was never robust. If petted much by his mother and sisters, he managed to enjoy himself in a manlier way with his boyish comrades, the pupil's of his father's school. This father was a Frenchman, transplanted from Nancy, and probably of Polish origin. Frédéric's mother, Justina Krzyzanowska, was, it need hardly be added, a pure Pole. For her the youthful pianist entertained a love that was characteristic. She became the leading motive of his life; all his actions were governed if not actually by her, at least in deference to her wishes. One of the things he feared most after he became a friend of the novelist, George Sand, was his mother's criticism. This trait, intensified later in life, was undoubtedly the reason for many of his actions. As he reverenced his mother, so he reverenced his mother's sex; and while his private life was not conventional, he always forbore from certain associations. Temperamentally the man had no taste for the things most prized by the world. He never married; he never gathered riches; and the honors heaped upon him as a virtuoso, the fame that greeted him almost at the tomb's portal, bore for him no message of joy. He was a dreamer of dreams.

Precocious musically, and sensitive as Mozart, Chopin early amused himself and his companions with his clever improvising. His father soon decided that there was a real gift to develop and engaged a Bohemian named Adalbert Zwyny to teach his son the rudiments of art. This instructor was a violinist as well as pianist and Chopin throve so well under his tutelage that he played a piano concerto by Gyrowetz in 1818 at a public concert and was more preoccupied with his new collar than with his success. "Everybody was looking at my collar," he remarked naïvely to his mother. The Polish aristocracy noted the gifts of the little fellow, participated in his education, and presently he began to study composition with Joseph Elsner, the chief influence for good in his musical career. Elsner was old fashioned but sound. He was a severe master and rigid in his discipline. If he gave the boy his own way in the matter of piano-playing, he never allowed him to relax in his study of the classics. Chopin many times referred with refreshing gratitude to his old master. And to him he owed all the sanity and lucidity of his music; it would have been an easy matter for the lad to have remained a brilliant improviser and rhapsodist. Elsner taught Chopin to cast his dreams into a durable mould.

Chopin's youth was spent if not happily, certainly not unpleasantly. He was in fairly good health, studied diligently without too great a strain upon his nerves, and doted much on his sisters. When at last he went to Vienna — he had been once as far as Berlin — great was the household's sorrow. He bravely lived it down, petted though he was, and actually tempted the fates by appealing to the suffrages of an elect Viennese audience August 11, 1829. On that occasion he played his Variations, Opus 2, on "*La ci darem la mano*" and several improvisations. His success was an unqualified one, and if he had followed it up it might have resulted in a permanent residence at Vienna. But after a second concert Chopin returned to Warsaw.

He had seen the world, had tasted of the fruit of knowledge, which in his case was not an evil fruit. On his return he fell promptly in love with

Constantia Gladowska, and who knows but his want of decision in declaring his passion was the cause of his second visit to Vienna! Certainly he became dispirited, and after two very flattering concerts in Warsaw he went to Breslau, Dresden and Prague, arriving in Vienna during the summer of 1831. Chopin had heard Rubini, the tenor, Henriette Sontag, the soprano, and being devoted to Italian singing, enjoyed as well as profited by their art. Hummel set him wild with enthusiasm and he must have envied Thalberg, then the lion pianist, for he speaks slightingly of him in his letters. Vienna was not so pleasant a place as formerly, for his friends, fearing the revolution, had gone to Germany and France. He soon left for Stuttgart and hearing of the capture of Warsaw by the Russians, September 8, 1831, wrote the Revolutionary Study in C minor, Opus 10, No. 12.

It was October, 1831, that Chopin first saw Paris, his home until the day of his death and the spot where now repose his remains. His career there was an eventful one for him, yet outwardly not rich in adventure. As in Warsaw the two determining factors of his life were his love for his mother and Constantia Gladowska so in Paris Chopin's nature expanded. He enjoyed social as well as artistic triumphs and he met George Sand. This was a happening of prime importance for him. The celebrated novelist had often boasted that she played the part of a stepmother to men of genius; that without her aid they might never have fully realized themselves. Be this as it may, Chopin's attachment to the fascinating woman became a part of his life. When at last they became bad friends, he drooped, withered, died. Sensitive he was to a morbid degree and he really passed from the care of his mother to that of George Sand. When she failed him, he could live no longer.

Such was the strange being who enchanted his hearers in the drawing-rooms of the French capital. A début at the house of Baron Rothschild decided his future. He became the "rage." Liszt admired him, finally adored him; and while Berlioz and Meyerbeer declared that he did not play in time — that is metronomically — they could not withhold their meed of praise. They simply could not comprehend his use of *tempo rubato* — a greatly misunderstood thing to-day. He was a phenomenon. Heine swore that Chopin was supernatural; and his charming spirituelle physiognomy and fairy-like playing certainly aided the illusion. Thalberg complained that his performances lacked weight, and this was no doubt the truth. For modern ears, accustomed to the heavy masses of orchestral tone that our virtuosi extort from their instruments, Chopin's liquid tones and gossamer flights would possibly seem unsubstantial. But there was the poet in his work. There was revealed a soul of tenderness and also the heroic soul. When he dashed into his fiery *Eroica* Polonaise he suggested the "cannons buried in flowers" as Schumann phrased it; when he sang with faint irony one of his capriciously perverse mazurkas his hearers divined that a new art, an art hitherto undreamed of, was being revealed. His was indeed a new art, with its employment of dispersed harmonies, novel use of the pedal, and dangerous rhythmic freedom. And this slender wonder-worker, the magician of all those spells, was constrained from public appearances because of his nervous timidity! It was his friend Liszt who fought in the musical arena and strangled lions with superb effrontery. Chopin's nature was too intimate—"the public suffocates me," he confessed.

Yet it must not be imagined that with all this delicacy of physique and temperament he was a sentimental, hectic dawdler. He labored over his compositions, filing for hours, days, weeks, and months at one piece. He gave many lessons, but saved no money. A few visits to England, a trip to the island of Majorca in the Mediterranean Sea with the Sand family, where he nearly perished of lung trouble, and his rupture with Madame Sand —this about comprises the history of Chopin. His life is writ large in his music. To it we must go to understand the man.

III

To make a viable selection from Chopin's music is a perilous task; it is a question of a little taken while great riches remain behind. Five Sonatas fairly set before us the many-sided Beethoven, yet a Ballade, Scherzo, Étude, Prelude, Valse, Sonata, Polonaise, Impromptu or Nocturne of Chopin will surely send us to the many other neglected ones of the same titles. Necessity is cruel, so the editor of a collection is compelled to sacrifice the more extended and difficult compositions, making his choice a representative rather than a complete one. Chopin was so versatile, he presented in so many disguises a single thought, that he ends by bewildering. The present edition is therefore an attempt to present the composer in his most favorable light. And this statement is not to be taken in an apologetic sense. For example, if necessary, the Scherzo in B minor, Opus 20, could have been included. But its relentless mocking spirit, its drastic irony may be found within the more confined walls of the B minor Mazurka. Nor is that overwhelming Polonaise in F sharp minor here, for technically it is only possible in the hands of a virtuoso. The editor has found that the E flat minor Polonaise, Opus 26, No. 2, contains in sufficient abundance the revolt, the fire and hatred of the later Polonaise. The other two Polonaises, in C sharp minor and A major, give a complete picture of Chopin's capricious melancholy and his martial vigor: indeed the A major Polonaise, surnamed the Military, is quite as heroic as the more celebrated one in A flat major, the Drum Polonaise.

This collection opens with the Preludes. These tiny, questioning tone-poems were composed by Chopin — some of them, not all — while he lay ailing at Majorca. The one in D flat is justly celebrated and it is called the Raindrop. Chopin, so relates Madame Sand, saw in a waking dream her and the two children drowned — she was absent during the progress of a storm, tropical in its severity — and it was the drip-drip of the rain upon the faces of the dead that sent the too imaginative poet shivering to his piano. Probably the dropping of rain through the dilapidated roof of his ancient abode on the island evoked the rhythmic foundation of this Prelude. The first Prelude should be repeated. The one in G with the running bass figure is very pretty in sentiment. And it must not be forgotten by the student that there are twenty-two other Preludes, all as beautiful.

The Nocturnes, chosen for their variety and wealth of mood, give us Chopin on his secret side. He loved the twilight more than the dawn — dreamers of his type do not rise early — and in the six Nocturnes we may find nearly all he had to say in this fascinating form. The Nocturne in F sharp is charged with feeling; yet it must not be delivered sentimentally. The one in D flat is very poetic, a companion piece for that in G major with its clinging double notes, its atmosphere of languorous reverie. The Nocturne in G minor is very popular. The second theme is said to be the transcription of monks chanting in some bare, ruined choir. The five Studies are the more pleasing, the technical problems being hidden by the graceful devices of the composer. The first one in G flat is familiar in the concert room and with its companion in the same key is very brilliant and effective. The Æolian Harp Study in A flat is another favorite; but the one in D flat deserves to be heard more frequently. It is a study in contrasted rhythms and *legato* and *staccato* touches. Sprightly, graceful, charming, this dainty piece repays careful study.

Out of many Mazurkas eight are chosen. In no form has Chopin manifested his originality as in these epigrammatic dances — they have been called Dances of the Soul. Variety in mood and tonality is duly considered. Thus opposed to the saucy Mazurka in B flat, the sad hesitancy of the one in B flat minor proves an admirable foil. The A minor Mazurka has that morbid flavor which betokens a soul weary of life; but the two in D flat and A flat are excellent antidotes. The Funeral March needs no comment here. It still remains mortuary music without rival. Nor does the Cradle Song, loveliest of its style, demand analysis. The two Impromptus are studies in contrast; the first all clarity, its outlines never blurred; the second is redolent of caprice and pessimism. With the A flat Ballade we come upon the larger forms of the master, a form specifically his own. In it his dramatic despair, his defiance to fate, his melting lyricism and his brilliant flights are felt. This Ballade is wonderful. It requires well-trained fingers and a bold heart to subdue it. The student must give especial study to pedaling and phrasing. "The pedal is the breath of the pianoforte."

The Polonaises have been mentioned. The Valses, too, demand no extended commentary. They range the gamut of the Warsaw Chopin to the Chopin of Paris. And they all dance. They are a veritable Dance of the Nerves. The more celebrated are the two in A flat, Opus 42, and C sharp minor, Opus 64, No. 2. The first and the last in A minor, Opus 34, and E minor [posthumous] exhale melancholy. But the one in D flat—named the Valse of the Little Dog—and those in G flat and A flat are delightful in their swinging rhythms and subtle avoidance of the banal accent. With the famous Scherzo in B flat minor the volume is complete. This Byronic poem full of fire, fury, and sweetness is the very epitome of Chopin's innermost nature. His was a haughty if shrinking soul and the hatred he felt for his country's oppressors mingled with his own sense of impotence—these opposing qualities gave birth to this magnificent work. The original connotation of Scherzo is jesting, but as Schumann justly asks: "How is Gravity to clothe itself if Jest goes about in dark veils?"

We may claim then that the forty numbers in this volume are fairly representative of Chopin's genius. Music such as the Barcarolle, the F minor Fantaisie, the Krakowiak or the Allegro de Concert is not for the amateur, so does not come within the scope of these selections. Various editions have been consulted for the fingering, phrasing, dynamics, pedaling, *tempi*, etc. All that the student requires for biographical or critical study of Chopin may be found in the comprehensive biography by Frederick Niecks, in Franz Liszt's brilliant monograph, in the Letters edited by Moritz Karosowski, in Henry T. Finck's "Chopin," and in the two small pamphlets entitled respectively: "The Works of Frédéric Chopin and their Proper Interpretation," and "Chopin's Greater Works." They are written by Jean Kleczynski of Warsaw.

James Huneker

THE CHOPIN PLAYER

The sounds torture me: I see them in my brain;
They spin a flickering web of living threads,
Like butterflies upon the garden beds,
Nets of bright sound. I follow them: in vain.
I must not brush the least dust from their wings:
They die of a touch; but I must capture them,
Or they will turn to a caressing flame,
And lick my soul up with their flutterings.

The sounds torture me: I count them with my eyes,
I feel them like a thirst between my lips;
Is it my body or my soul that cries
With little colored mouths of sound, and drips
In these bright drops that turn to butterflies
Dying delicately at my finger tips?

ARTHUR SYMONS

Frédéric Chopin is the proudest poetic spirit of
  his time.   ROBERT SCHUMANN

FORTY PIANO COMPOSITIONS
BY FRÉDÉRIC CHOPIN

A Mr J.C. Kessler

PRELUDE, in C

★ (September 1839)

FRÉDÉRIC CHOPIN
Op. 28, No 1

★ Throughout the volume the given dates are those of publication.

À Mr J. C. Kessler

PRELUDE, in G
(September 1839)

FRÉDÉRIC CHOPIN
Op. 28, N.º 3

A M.r J.C. Kessler

PRELUDE, in D Flat
(THE RAINDROP)
(September 1839)

FRÉDÉRIC CHOPIN
Op. 28, N.º 15

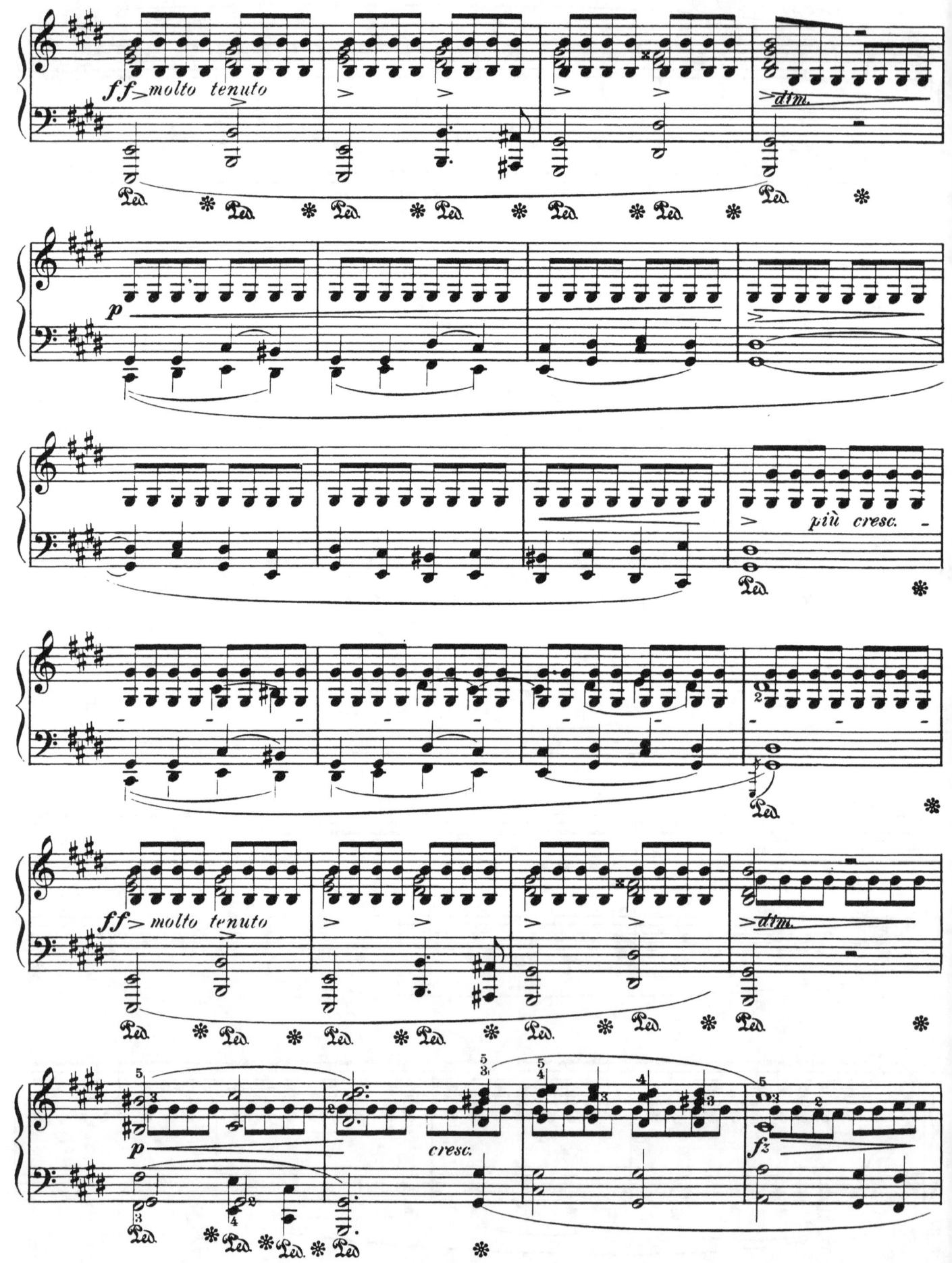

À M.r Johns, de la Nouvelle Orléans

MAZURKA, in B Flat

(November 1834)

FRÉDÉRIC CHOPIN
Op. 7, N°1

A M.r le Comte de Perthuis

MAZURKA, in B Flat Minor

(January 1836)

FRÉDÉRIC CHOPIN
Op. 24, N.º 4

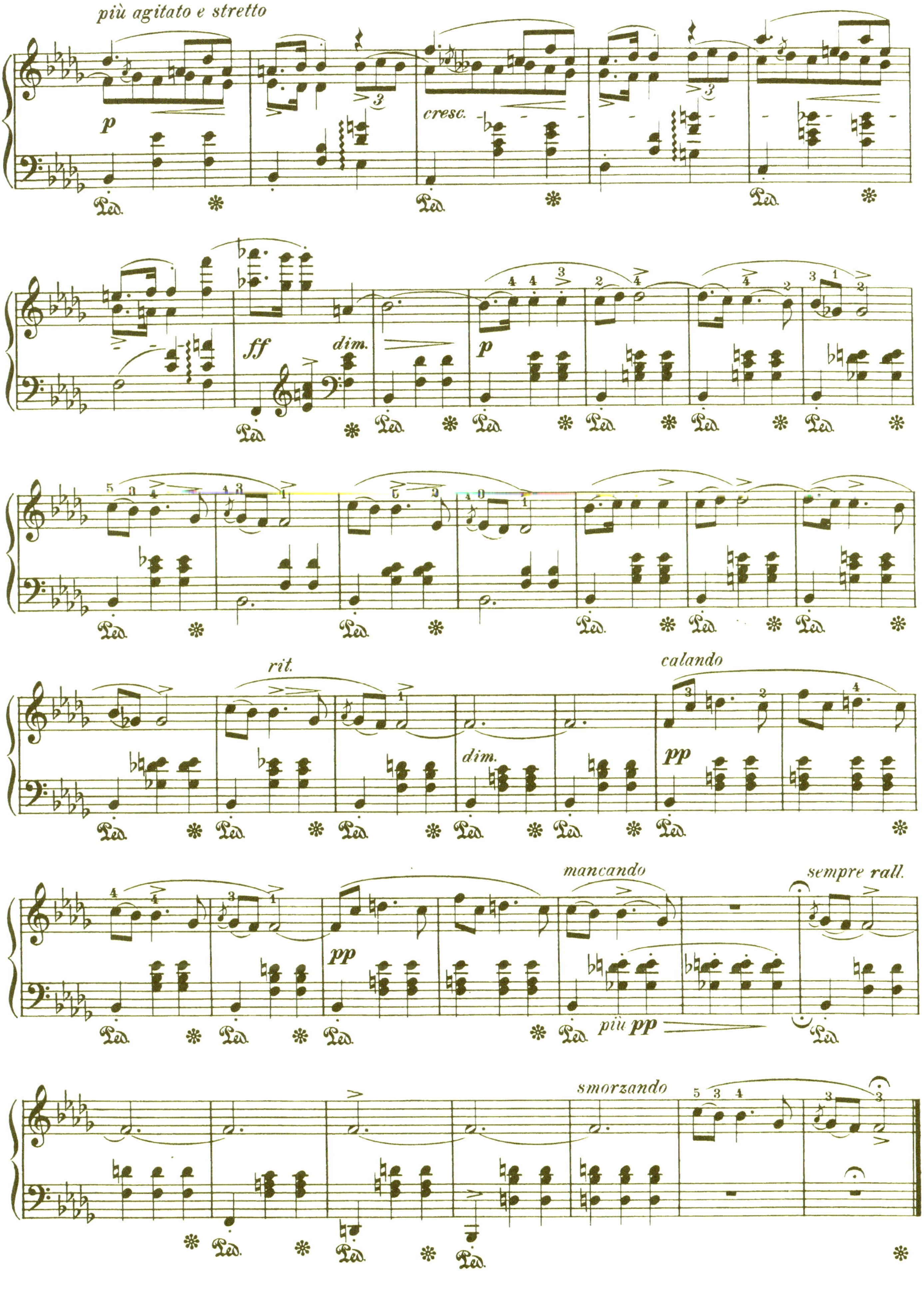
più agitato e stretto
p
cresc.
ff
dim.
p
rit.
dim.
calando
pp
mancando
sempre rall.
pp
più pp
smorzando

MAZURKA, in D Flat

(January 1838)

FRÉDÉRIC CHOPIN
Op. 30, N° 3

Allegro non troppo

À Mlle la Comtesse Mostowska

MAZURKA, in C
(November 1838)

FRÉDÉRIC CHOPIN
Op. 33, N°3

A Mlle la Comtesse Mostowska

MAZURKA, in B Minor

(November 1838)

FRÉDÉRIC CHOPIN
Op. 33, N° 4

A Mr. Léon Szmitkowski

MAZURKA, in A Flat
(September 1842)

FREDERIC CHOPIN
Op. 50, No 2

28

MAZURKA, in A Minor

(Posthumous)

(1827)

FREDERIC CHOPIN
Op. 68, No. 2

Lento (♩= 116)

À Madame la Comtesse d'Agoult

STUDY, in A Flat
(THE ÆOLIAN HARP)

(October 1837)

FRÉDÉRIC CHOPIN
Op. 25, No. 1

À Madame la Comtesse d'Agoult
STUDY, in C sharp Minor
(October 1837)

FRÉDERIC CHOPIN
Op. 25, No. 7

44

STUDY, in G Flat
(THE BUTTERFLY)

A Madame la Comtesse d'Agoult

(October 1837)

FRÉDÉRIC CHOPIN
Op. 25, No. 9

STUDY, in D Flat

(Nº 3 of the Three Studies composed for the "Method" of Moscheles and Fétis)

(September 1840)

FRÉDÉRIC CHOPIN

À Mr Ferdinand Hiller

NOCTURNE, in F Sharp

(January 1834)

FRÉDÉRIC CHOPIN
Op.15, No 2

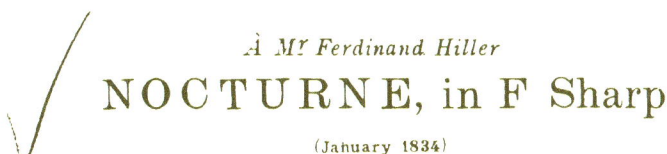

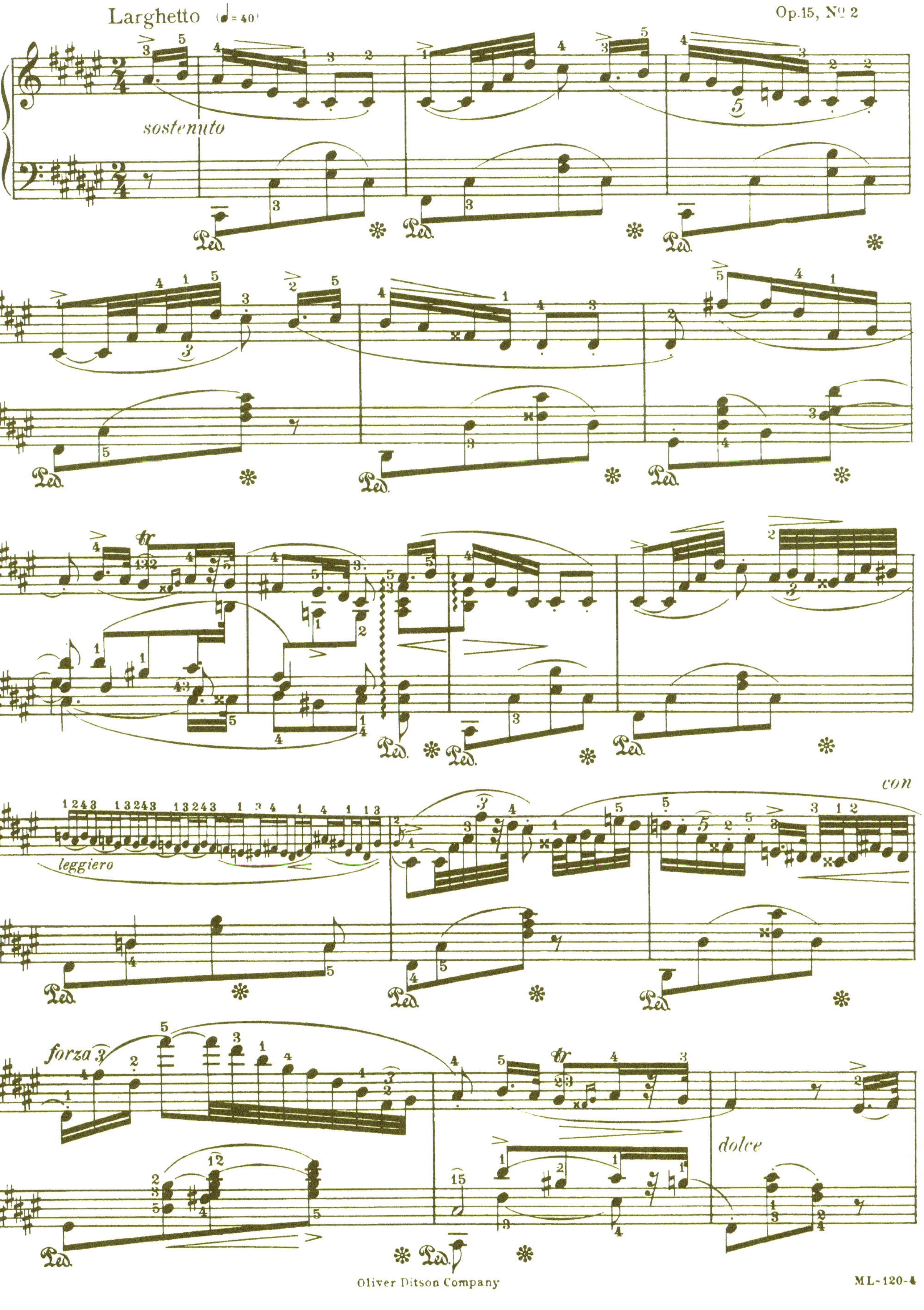

Oliver Ditson Company
ML-120-4

À Mme la Comtesse d'Appony

NOCTURNE, in D Flat

(July 1836)

FRÉDÉRIC CHOPIN.
Op. 27, No 2

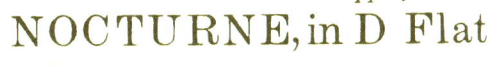

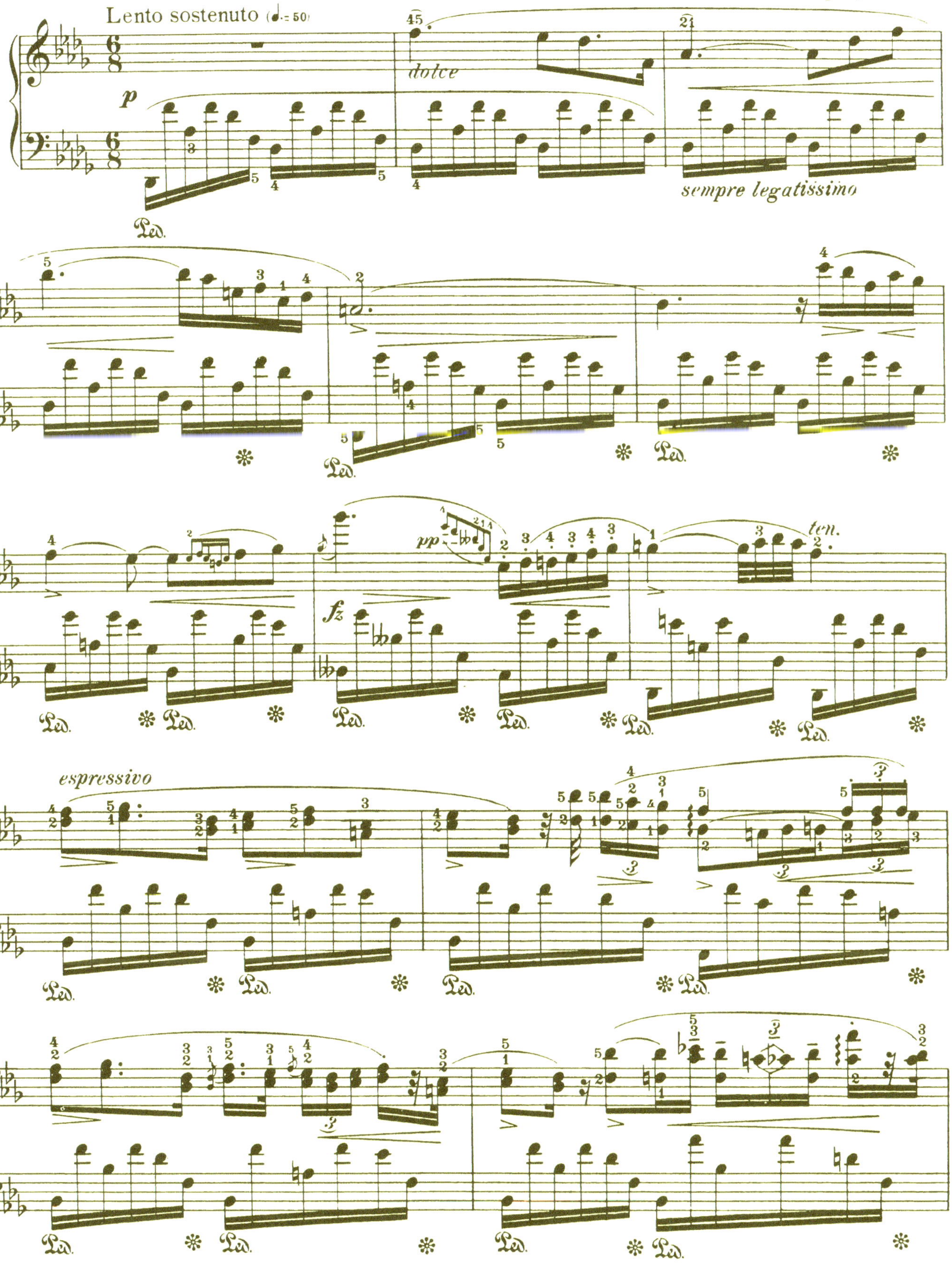

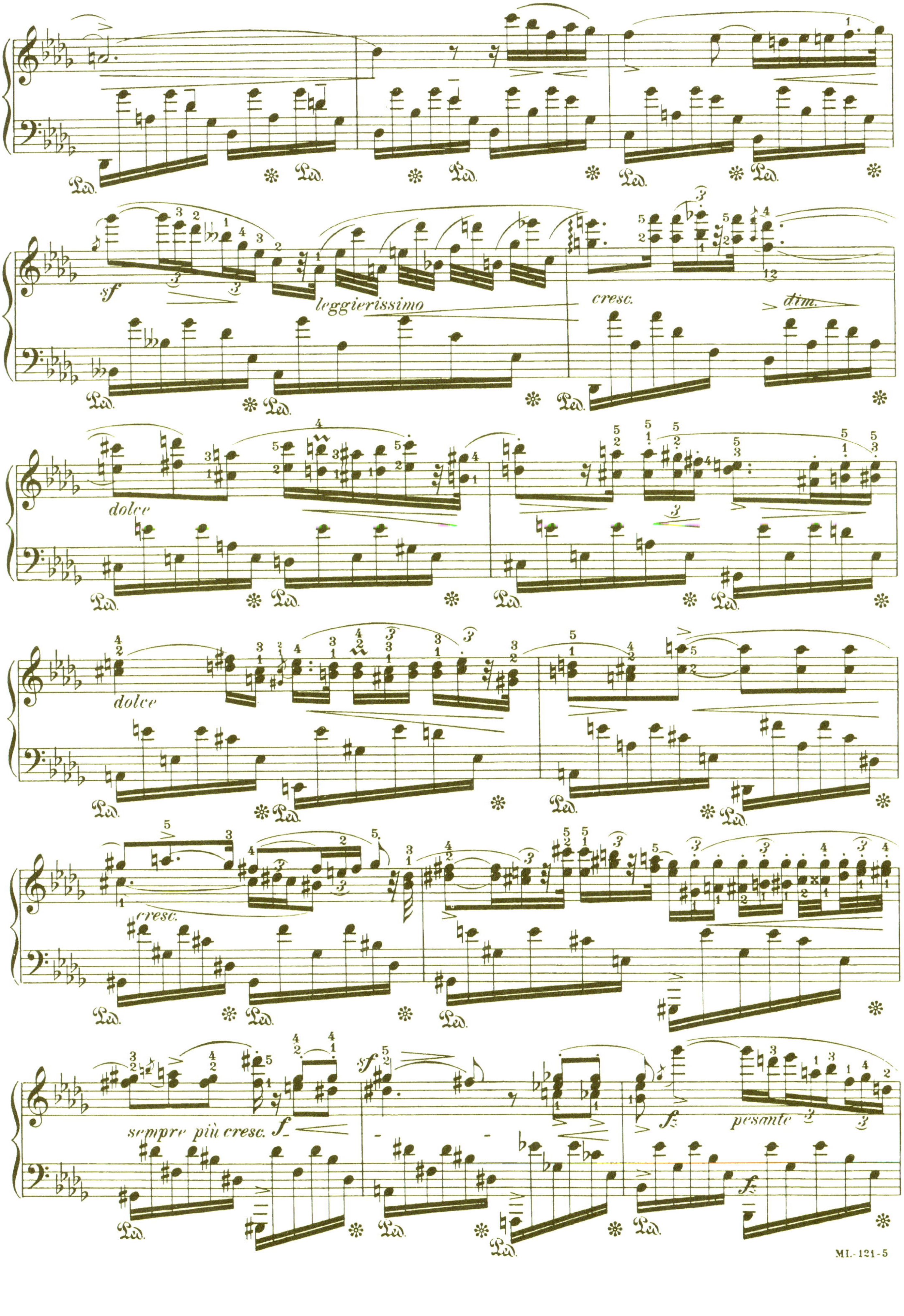
sf
leggierissimo
cresc.
dim.
dolce
dolce
cresc.
sempre più cresc. f
sf
f
pesante

NOCTURNE, in B Major

À M.me la Baronne de Billing

(December 1837)

FRÉDÉRIC CHOPIN
Op. 32 N.º 1

NOCTURNE, in G Minor

(May 1840)

FRÉDÉRIC CHOPIN
Op. 37, No. 1

Andante sostenuto

Oliver Ditson Company

NOCTURNE, in G

(June 1840)

FRÉDÉRIC CHOPIN
Op. 37, No 2

A Mlle de Thun-Hohenstein

VALSE BRILLANTE, in A Flat

(December 1838)

FRÉDÉRIC CHOPIN
Op. 34, N° 1

À Madame G. d'Ivry

VALSE, in A Minor
(December 1837)

FRÉDÉRIC CHOPIN
Op. 34, N.º 2

Oliver Ditson Company

GRANDE VALSE, in A Flat

(July 1840)

FRÉDÉRIC CHOPIN
Op 42

102

A Mme la Comtesse Delphine Potocka

VALSE, in D Flat
(October 1847)

FRÉDÉRIC CHOPIN
Op. 64, No 1

A Mme la Baronne de Rothschild

VALSE, in C sharp Minor
(1847)

FRÉDÉRIC CHOPIN
Op. 64, No 2

À Mme la Baronne Katharina Bronicka

VALSE, in A Flat

(1847)

FRÉDÉRIC CHOPIN
Op. 64, N° 3

VALSE, in E Minor
(Posthumous)

FRÉDÉRIC CHOPIN

122

POLONAISE, in C sharp Minor

À Mr J. Dessauer

(July 1836)

Allegro appassionato

FRÉDÉRIC CHOPIN
Op. 26, N° 1

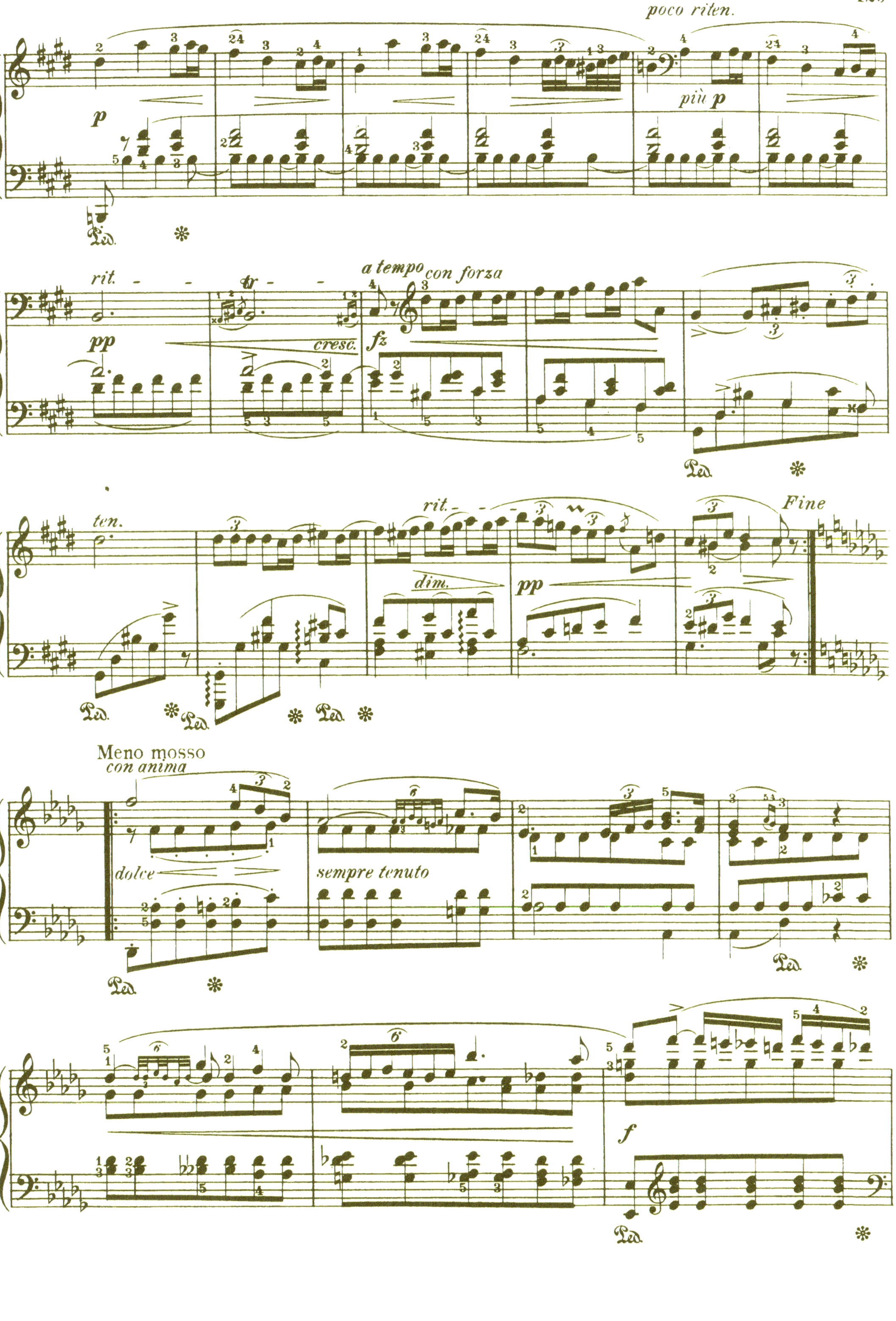
poco riten.
più p
rit.
cresc.
a tempo
con forza
ten.
rit.
dim.
Fine
Meno mosso
con anima
dolce
sempre tenuto

130

131

132

À Mlle la Comtesse de Lobau

IMPROMPTU I

(December 1837)

FRÉDÉRIC CHOPIN
Op. 29

Allegro assai, quasi presto

Oliver Ditson Company

FANTAISIE - IMPROMPTU

(Posthumous. Composed about 1834)

FRÉDÉRIC CHOPIN
Op. 66

144

BALLADE III

À Mlle Pauline de Noailles

(January 1842)

FRÉDÉRIC CHOPIN
Op. 47

150

156

A Mlle la Comtesse A. de Fürstenstein

SCHERZO II, in B Flat Minor
(February 1838)

FRÉDÉRIC CHOPIN
Op. 31

Oliver Ditson Company

162

168

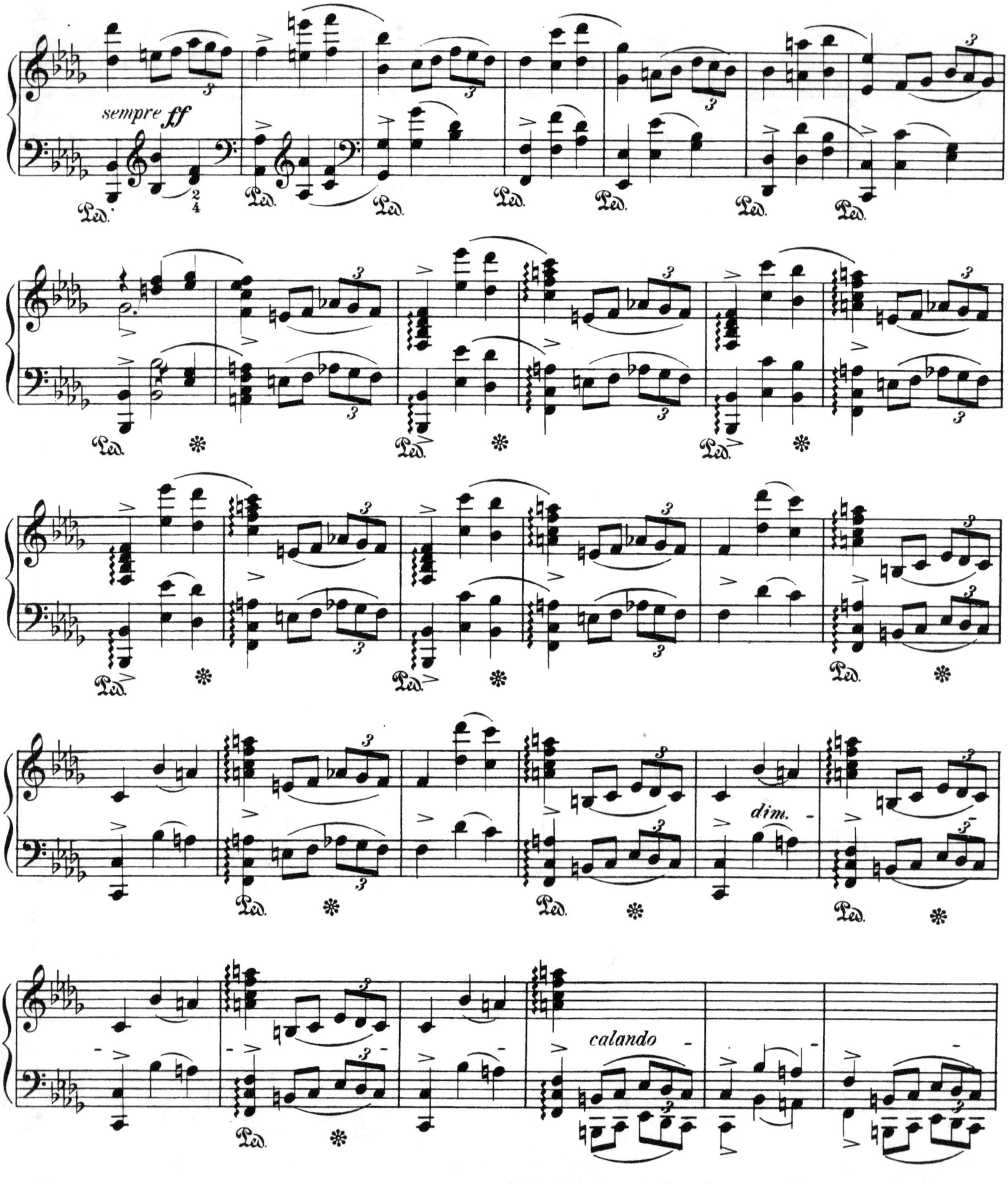
sempre ff
dim.
calando
smorzando

À Mlle Elise Gavard

BERCEUSE
(June 1845)

FRÉDÉRIC CHOPIN
Op. 57

176

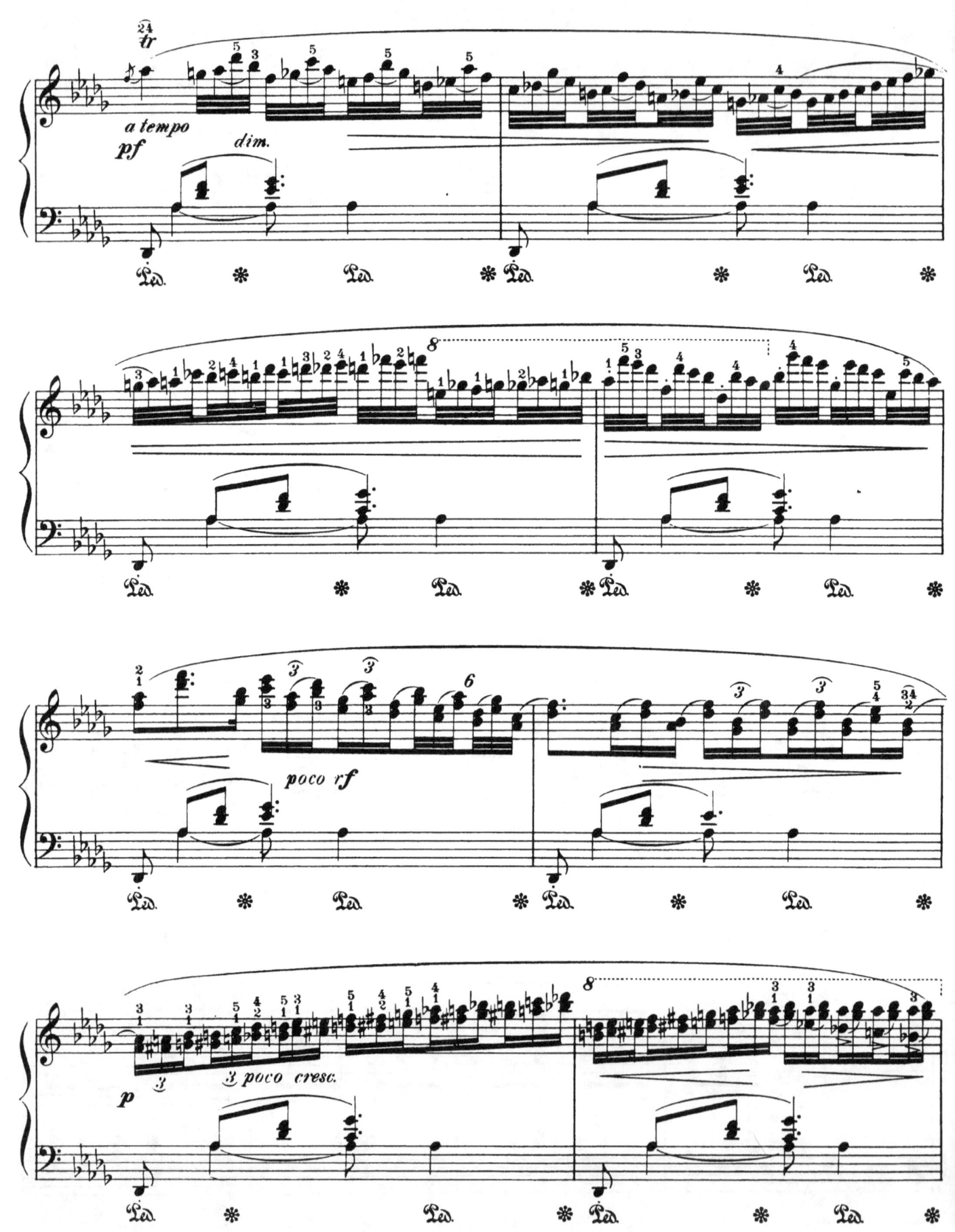

178

FUNERAL MARCH
(MARCHE FUNÈBRE)

(May, 1840)

FRÉDÉRIC CHOPIN,
From the Sonata Op. 35, No. 2

Grade V

Oliver Ditson Company

M.L.-140-4

182